CATS SET IV

SOMALI CATS

Nancy Furstinger
ABDO Publishing Company

visit us at
www.abdopub.com

Published by ABDO Publishing Company, 4940 Viking Drive, Edina, Minnesota 55435.
Copyright © 2006 by Abdo Consulting Group, Inc. International copyrights reserved in
all countries. No part of this book may be reproduced in any form without written
permission from the publisher. The Checkerboard Library™ is a trademark and logo of
ABDO Publishing Company.

Printed in the United States.

Cover Photo: Corbis
Interior Photos: Animals Animals pp. 9, 19; Corbis pp. 5, 7, 15; Peter Arnold pp. 12, 17,
    20, 21; Ron Kimball pp. 6, 11, 13

Series Coordinator: Megan Murphy
Editors: Heidi M. Dahmes, Megan Murphy
Art Direction: Neil Klinepier

Library of Congress Cataloging-in-Publication Data

Furstinger, Nancy.
    Somali cats / Nancy Furstinger.
        p. cm. -- (Cats. Set IV)
    Includes bibliographical references.
    ISBN 1-59679-268-X
        1. Somali cat--Juvenile literature. I. Title.

SF449.S65.F87 2006
636.8'3--dc22
                                                            2005041091

CONTENTS

LIONS, TIGERS, AND CATS

Around 3,500 years ago, ancient Egyptians began welcoming wildcats into their homes as pets. These cats hunted rats and mice that feasted on grains stored in silos. Egyptians believed cats were sacred and often worshipped them in temples.

Domestic cats can trace their roots back to these African wildcats. Today, cats continue to be cherished as family members. More than 40 different **breeds** of domestic cats exist worldwide. They come in assorted colors, shapes, and sizes.

All cats belong to the **Felidae** family. This family contains 38 different species, including lions, tigers, cheetahs, and panthers.

While it is common for cats to dislike water, some members of the Felidae family actually enjoy playing in it.

SOMALI CATS

Somali cats are a fairly new **breed**. They were only introduced within the past 40 years. However, their closest relative is the Abyssinian. This is one of the oldest **domestic** cat breeds in the world.

Somalis are similar to Abyssinians in every way except hair length. Abyssinians are a short-haired breed. Throughout history, long-haired kittens appeared in Abyssinian **litters**. These gifts of nature surprised Abyssinian breeders.

An Abyssinian

In the 1960s, **breeders** decided to take these long-haired Abyssinian kittens and create a new breed. American breeder Evelyn Mague named the breed Somali.

The first Somalis were born in the

The Cat Fanciers' Association (CFA) recognized the Somali breed in 1979. The CFA is a group that sets the standards for judging all breeds of cats.

United States. But since Somalis are so similar to Abyssinians, breeders decided to name this cat after Somalia. Somalia is the African nation that bordered Abyssinia. Abyssinia is now called Ethiopia.

QUALITIES

Somalis are smart, sociable cats that need a lot of attention. They love the outdoors and should not be confined or left alone for long periods of time. Somalis get along well with other pets, too.

Somalis show a lively interest in everything. They often open cabinets and drawers. Sometimes, they will carry objects around in their mouth. They have also been known to eat things they shouldn't.

Somalis are active and playful. They love toys and playing fetch. These cats will even invent their own games! They also like water. A dripping faucet is sure to attract this **breed**.

Opposite page: *Somalis have a very quiet voice and don't meow often.*

COAT AND COLOR

Somalis are actually considered a semi-longhaired cat. Their soft, silky hair is medium length. It appears longer around the neck, hindquarters, and tail. But, the hair is shorter on the shoulders and body.

The Somali's fur is flecked with ticking. A ticked coat has a base color that is interrupted by two to three bands of darker color. Also, the back of the Somali's hind legs and its paw pads are always darker than the coat.

Somalis can be blue, fawn, red, or ruddy. Silver coats are sometimes recognized, too. Tufts of hair grow in the ears and between the toes. The letter M marks the forehead.

Some people think Somalis look like foxes because of their reddish coloring, large ears, and bushy tail.

SIZE

The Somali is a medium-sized cat with a lean, muscular body. Like the Abyssinian, the Somali is more finely boned than other **breeds**. Males usually weigh more than females.

The Somali has a slightly arched back, and it looks like it walks on tiptoe. This cat's legs are long and slim. And the tail is bushy, like a fox's.

The curious, lively nature of the Somali makes it a perfect show cat. These cats always seem to know when they need to perform.

The Somali has a wedge-shaped head and a full **muzzle**. Large, flared ears and a masked face add to this cat's foxlike appearance. Big, almond-shaped eyes glow green or gold.

The ruddy color of this Somali is the most common coat color. The rich, golden brown undercoat is ticked with black.

CARE

Somali cats don't need a lot of grooming. Occasional attention with a bristle brush will remove loose hair and prevent matting. You can also run a comb through the longer fur on its neck and tail. But be gentle, so as not to break the hair.

This **breed** is energetic and bold. It will play with anything. Make sure it has plenty of toys to entertain itself. A scratching post allows your Somali to sharpen its claws. Plus, it keeps your cat from scratching furniture and clawing carpets.

Your Somali will need a **litter box**, too. Cats have a natural instinct to bury their waste. So, it won't take long to train them to use a litter box. Keep the box in a private place away from its food and water. And, remember to clean it daily!

The Somali is considered a healthy, hardy **breed**. Once a year, your cat will need to visit the veterinarian for a checkup and **vaccines**. The veterinarian can also **neuter** or **spay** your pet.

Somalis are active cats. And, they maintain a kittenish curiosity their entire lives!

FEEDING

Feed your Somali the same diet it ate at the **breeder**'s house. You can slowly mix in a new brand of food later. A gradual change will prevent your cat from getting an upset stomach.

Cats are meat eaters by nature. So, they need a source of protein in their diets, such as fish, beef, or chicken. Commercial cat food usually contains all the **nutrients** your cat needs.

There are three kinds of commercial cat food. They are dry, semimoist, and canned. Read the label to make sure that the food is suited to your cat's needs. The label will tell you how much to feed your pet based on its age, weight, and health.

Serve food and fresh, clean water in stainless steel bowls. While many kittens crave milk, some adult cats are unable to digest it.

These Somali kittens lick their chops after a meal. There are special kinds of commercial cat food for felines less than one year old.

KITTENS

Female Somali cats are loving mothers. They are **pregnant** for about 63 to 65 days. Somalis typically have **litters** of one to four kittens.

Kittens are born blind and deaf. Somali kittens are born with dark coats that gradually lighten as they get older. However, it can take up to two years for their full coat color to be established.

At first, kittens only drink their mother's milk. But by three weeks of age, they can try eating soft food. They also begin to wrestle and play with their brothers and sisters. Kittens can join their new families when they are 12 weeks old.

The Somali breed developed when people began breeding the long-haired kittens that appeared in short-haired Abyssinian litters.

Buying a Kitten

Somali cats are growing in popularity. If this cat captivates you, first do your homework on the **breed**. Visit breeders to inspect and play with their **purebred** kittens. Make certain that this energetic, attention-grabbing cat is for you.

Some breed rescues or veterinary clinics might have Somali cats for adoption. These cats love company, so consider adopting a friend for your feline! A healthy Somali can live more than 15 years.

Somalis are a sweet, affectionate breed.

It is important to cat-proof your home before adopting this breed. Somalis find ways to get into everything. And, they often eat things they shouldn't!

GLOSSARY

breed - a group of animals sharing the same appearance and characteristics. A breeder is a person who raises animals. Raising animals is often called breeding them.

domestic - animals that are tame.

Felidae - the scientific Latin name for the cat family.

litter - all of the kittens born at one time to a mother cat.

litter box - a box filled with cat litter, which is similar to sand. Cats use litter boxes to dispose of their waste.

muzzle - an animal's nose and jaws.

neuter (NOO-tuhr) - to remove a male animal's reproductive organs.

nutrient - a substance found in food and used in the body to promote growth, maintenance, and repair.

pregnant - having one or more babies growing within the body.

purebred - an animal whose parents are both from the same breed.

spay - to remove a female animal's reproductive organs.

vaccine (vak-SEEN) - a shot given to animals or humans to prevent them from getting an illness or disease.

WEB SITES

To learn more about Somali cats, visit ABDO Publishing Company on the World Wide Web at **www.abdopub.com**. Web sites about these cats are featured on our Book Links page. These links are routinely monitored and updated to provide the most current information available.

INDEX